HISTORIC PUBS

new south wales

CRAIG LEWIS AND SIMON PUNCH

BOILING BILLY
PUBLICATIONS

www.boilingbilly.com.au

CONTENTS

INTRODUCTION

The pub has been an integral part of New South Wales' history since the days of European settlement. At first these early grog shanties which sprung up in Sydney Town were often little more than a tent, serving rum, and at times, some type of concoction which was passed off as ale. With the progress of time more substantial buildings were constructed to act as pubs, and, as the population began to push further afield, both up and down the coast and over the Blue Mountains, pubs sprang up to help slake the thirst of those early pioneers. So began our tradition of the pub.

We've curated a selection of what we believe to be 25 of the more characterful historic inns and hotels in New South Wales. Some offered a welcoming cool refreshment after a hard day's work, such as Sydney's Lord Dudley Hotel which was frequented by local quarrymen. Others, such as Booroorban's Royal Mail Hotel provided travellers with meals and accommodation, and more often than not, most were places for community to meet and converse. To this day many possess a quality which is hard to put your finger on - is it their simplicity, atmosphere, charm or quirkiness?

Snippets of local history, such as the enduring legend of Harry Littlefair and his miner's lamp at The Neath Hotel bring these historic pubs to life. Yarns - both tall and true - abound in these characterful establishments, some having persisted for well over a century or more. So, was the Black Stump Hotel in Merriwagga really named for a teamster's wife who was burnt to death at a camp near the town? And, does the ghost of a young labourer tragically killed in a mine disaster still haunt the cellar of the Mount Kembla Hotel?

Some of New South Wales' best historic pubs are waiting here for you to discover. We hope you enjoy the experience.

Craig Lewis and Simon Punch 2018

BELLBROOK HOTEL

bellbrook, macleay valley

Built in 1913 of local hardwood clad with weatherboards, the Bellbrook Hotel was considered a large establishment for its day and location, originally comprising of 15 rooms. The pub, which is perched on a bank above the Macleay River, still retains much of its early character, both inside and out.

The area was settled in the 1830s by timber cutters in search of red cedar and graziers who took up squatting licences. The hotel, along with the rest of the small Bellbrook township, is now heritage listed as an example of an early 1900s timber getting town.

To many Bellbrook is the birthplace of Australian country music and is the childhood home of country music legend Slim Dusty. The homestead where Slim grew up is nearby and can be visited. *CL*

Bellbrook is located 470km from Sydney via the Pacific Highway and 45km north-west of Kempsey on the Kempsey to Armidale Road. The drive from Kempsey, which follows the Macleay River, takes about an hour.

☎ 02 6567 2071 🌐 www.bellbrookhotel.com.au

BLACK STUMP HOTEL

---

merriwagga, northern riverina

The Black Stump Hotel was built in 1926 and at 1.31 metres, boasts the tallest bar in the Southern Hemisphere. Nearly everyone sits on stools, most notably the more vertically challenged! Legend attests that the oak bar was built to this height to accommodate patrons who didn't want to dismount from their horse to enjoy a drink. Whether this is true or not, it's a good yarn.

The only pub in the tiny Riverina settlement of Merriwagga, it is said the hotel takes its name from an 1880s tragedy when the wife of a bullock teamster was burnt to death. Apparently, her dress had caught alight by the evening campfire at a waterhole not far from town. Found by her husband upon returning to camp after tending his animals, the husband, in the rather dry matter-of-factness of the Australian bushman, told police that when he found her she "looked just like a black stump".

The hotel offers both meals and accomodation. *CL*

Merriwagga is 75km north-west of Griffith and 40km south of Hillston via the Kidman Way. The Black Stump Hotel is on the corner of Aix Street and Mons Street.

☎ 02 6965 4457 🌐 www.blackstumphotel.blogspot.com.au

BUSHRANGER HOTEL

---

collector, southern highlands

First established in 1860 as the Commercial Hotel, this charming stone pub was also known as Kimberley's Inn until taking on the name of The Bushranger Hotel. In days long gone Collector boasted five inns, but now only one remains.

The pub takes its name from the notorious bushranger Ben Hall and his gang of Johnny Gilbert and John Dunn. On January 26th, 1865 the gang rode into town and raided the hotel. In the ruckus the town's policeman, Constable Samuel Nelson was shot dead by Dunn. Dunn was later hung for the murder.

Built from locally quarried stone, the hotel comprises three levels: bars and dining on the ground floor, rooms and amenities on the second floor and a loft above, which would have originally been the publican's sleeping quarters. *SP*

Collector lies just off the Federal Highway, 35km south-west from Goulburn and 55km north-east of Canberra. The hotel is on Church Street and a monument to Constable Nelson stands beside the pub.

☎ 02 4848 0071 🌐 www.thebushrangerhotel.com.au

THIS PAGE: The front bar is the focal point of the Bushranger Hotel. The timber lining boards on the wall frame a collection of artefacts and curios which have been collected from around the region, including a cross-cut saw, wild dog traps, assorted pieces of bushranging memorabilia and historic photographs. At one time a pistol, allegedly belonging to bushranger Ben Hall, was on display in the pub, but it has long since disappeared.

ABOVE: Old beer cans, such as this vintage Reschs Draught tin can, adorn shelves scattered around the hotel.

RIGHT: When Collector's Lockup Keeper, Constable Samuel Nelson was called to investigate the arrival of Hall's Gang in town, he was confronted by John Dunn, who demanded he 'stand'. Nelson continued to advance and was shot by Dunn in the chest and again in the head. One of Nelson's sons witnessed his father's death and was then shot at by Dunn, before escaping. After the shooting, gang member Gilbert came out of Kimberley's Inn and took Nelson's belt and carbine, who lay dead outside the pub. This monument to Nelson was unveiled in February 1908 and sits beside the hotel.

CROSS ROADS HOTEL

tomingley, central west

The Cross Roads Hotel was first established in 1880 during a gold rush to the area. During these short-lived but busy times it was one of two pubs open for trade. The village of Tomingley serviced five goldmines and boasted three stores, a public school as well as the two hotels.

Today, wheat, sheep and cattle farming are the area's main industries. The current Cross Roads Hotel was rebuilt in 1940. The single storey brick pub sports an L-shaped bar equipped with old coolroom doors, an open fireplace, pool table and, like many bush pubs, has a dining room out the back. *SP*

Tomingley is situated roughly 50km south-west of Dubbo on the Newell Highway, which is the main route for truckies heading between Brisbane and Melbourne. Peak Hill is about 20km south and Parkes another 50km further on, also via the Newell Highway.

☎ **02 6869 3219** 🌐 **www.facebook.com/CrossRoadsHotelTomingley**

DROMEDARY HOTEL

central tilba, far south coast

Nestled in the shadow of Gulaga, or Mother Mountain to the local Yuin people, is the picture perfect village of Central Tilba. Gulaga was given the name of Mount Dromedary by Captain Cook as he sailed past in April 1770, he likened it to a camel, or dromedary's hump.

The charming Dromedary Hotel, which sits in the centre of the village, was built in 1895 for Jim Livingstone as a coffee palace, going by the name of The Palace Hotel. The hotel was renamed shortly after the end of World War II, taking its current name from nearby Mount Dromedary.

The hotel is perched on the high side of the street and walking through the door there are a plethora of historic pictures scattered throughout the main bar area, which has a cosy feel. There is a dining area and beer garden out the back while the downstairs front verandah is a popular spot to watch the comings and goings in town. Upstairs offers three guestrooms. The two storey weatherboard hotel is heritage-listed.*CL*

Central Tilba is just off the Princes Highway and 20km south of Narooma, while Bega is just under 60km to the south.

☎ **02 4473 7223** 🌐 **www.facebook.com/Dromedary-Hotel**

FORTUNE OF WAR HOTEL

---

the rocks, sydney

The Fortune of War lays claim to being Sydney's oldest continually licensed pub. Built by emancipated convict Samuel Terry and first licensed in 1828, it was originally constructed of sandstone until Tooth & Co brewers rebuilt the hotel of brick in the early 1920s after acquiring the licence.

The hotel has had a long association with Australian military personnel, providing last drinks for many who boarded the ships at Circular Quay, heading to overseas conflicts and first drinks for those who returned.

While the current building doesn't really do 'Sydney's Oldest Pub' title any justice, its age resonates upon the walls inside and at the U-shaped ornate Edwardian styled bar. The upstairs bar displays pictures of the twelve First Fleet ships and their manifests, while in the main George Street bar lawyers rub shoulders with tradies, and long-time locals mingle with world-travelled tourists. *SP*

The Fortune Of War is situated in The Rocks, Sydney. The Pub is at 137 George Street, about 800 metres north of Wynyard train station and literally a hop, skip and a jump from Circular Quay.

☎ 02 9247 2714 🌐 www.fortuneofwar.com.au

GOLD AND FLEECE HOTEL

windeyer, central west

During the latter part of the 1850s and early years of the 1860s, Windeyer was New South Wales' largest goldmining community. Then known as Richardsons Point and being a 'tent town', it saw little in the way of permanence as miners moved from field to field. The Great Depression of the 1930s saw a renewed, but short-lived interest in the goldfields as hopefuls scoured the old mullock heaps.

The present timber hotel, which touts itself as 'a quintessential country pub', was relocated from Queensland in 1911 and originally operated as the Commercial Hotel. In the 1970s the pub was renamed the Gold and Fleece Hotel, most probably as a nod to the area's past goldmining prosperity and its now well-deserved reputation as a producer of fine merino wool.

Through the front door is a spacious bar room featuring local memorabilia. The ceiling is of decorative pressed metal. *CL*

Windeyer is located 260km north-west of Sydney via the Great Western Highway and Castlereagh Highway. The village is 43km south-west of Mudgee via the Hill End and Windeyer roads.

☎ 02 6373 8383 ⊕ www.windeyerhotel.weebly.com

GREAT WESTERN HOTEL

cobar, outback

A landmark standing proudly in the centre of Cobar's main street for well over 100 years, the handsome two storey Great Western Hotel is hard to miss. Boasting the longest iron-lace verandah in New South Wales, the hotel was established in 1898 by Pierce Goold. A man of many talents - businessman, mining company director and a qualified accountant - Goold left Cobar to fight in World War I and was killed at Gallipoli in 1915.

Considered a classic example of a traditional rural Australian corner pub, it was originally constructed as a single storey structure and extended to a second storey in 1903.

Downstairs contains the bars and restaurant while a timber staircase leads upstairs to guestrooms lining the long hallway and out onto the famous 100m long timber verandah. Elegant promenades and foot races were once held on the verandah during Cobar's heyday. *SP*

Cobar is a little over 700km north-west from Sydney and lies at the crossroads of the Kidman Way and Barrier Highway. It's roughly 132km east to Nyngan, 260km west to Wilcannia and Bourke is about 160km north.

☏ **02 6836 2503** ⊕ **www.facebook.com/GreatWesternHotelMotel**

HERO OF WATERLOO HOTEL

the rocks, sydney

The legendary Hero of Waterloo Hotel has a grand history dating back to 1843. While only missing out on the title of Sydney's oldest pub by a couple of years, it is evident when you walk inside that not a lot has changed since the pub's foundation times. Constructed of sandstone in 1843 by George Paton, the hotel is built in a unique triangular shape.

Entering the hotel into the main bar, the ceilings are held high by huge timber beams while the long, wooden bar is filled with characters young and old, local and not. Up on the split ground floor is a dining room while a wooden staircase leads to the upstairs restaurant. Downstairs is a cellar hewn out of sandstone.

The hotel is rumoured to be haunted and it is thought to be the ghost of Anne Kirkman, a former publican's wife who was pushed down the stairs by her husband in 1849. *SP*

The Hero of Waterloo is in Sydney's historic Rocks precinct on the corner of Lower Fort Street and Windmill Street, just a short stroll from the Lord Nelson Hotel. It is a pleasant walk from Circular Quay where there are trains, ferries and buses.

☎ 02 9252 4553   ⊕ www.heroofwaterloo.com.au

ABOVE: Down in the pub's cellar there is an underground tunnel, which apparently lead to Sydney Harbour around Walsh Bay. This tunnel, which has since been blocked, was rumoured to have been used to smuggle rum and for the involuntary recruitment of sailors. One too many drinks and you could find yourself sailing the seven seas! The cellar was also used as a lockup for convicts while their keepers imbibed a quiet ale upstairs.

LEFT: The convict-hewn sandstone used to build the hotel was taken from the nearby Argyle Cut. The Argyle Cut - a tunnel partly hewn by convict wielded picks through solid sandstone - was constructed to provide direct access between Millers Point and The Rocks. Each block used in the hotel has its own unique chiselled-pattern so the convicts could distinguish their work to meet their daily quota. If you look closely some of the stones have initials, which are said to be those of the convicts who cut them.

THIS PAGE: Today, the Hero of Waterloo is one of 14 hotels scattered throughout Millers Point and was once a favoured hostelry for the military garrison stationed nearby. Much of the hotel's interior remains faithful to its past, including the pub's bar and cellar. The pub takes its name from the Irish-born Duke of Wellington, best known for his feats against Napoleon Bonaparte at the Battle of Waterloo in 1815. Wellington went on to become Prime Minister of Great Britain in 1828.

LAGGAN HOTEL

---

laggan, southern tablelands

Originally named The Laggan Inn, the single storey weatherboard hotel was first licensed around 1860. The original Inn building was destroyed by fire and rebuilt beside the hotel's original site in 1924.

The Hart family purchased the pub in 1947 and it still remains in the family today, now run by daughter Margaret and husband Ron Campbell. This quintessential country pub exudes a charm, character and friendliness that is often lost in today's frenetic society.

The hotel features a cosy double-sided main bar, dining room, two accommodation rooms, rustic country gardens out back and a tennis court. The bar walls and ceiling are adorned with memorabilia including pictures of locally breed prize-winning cattle and sheep for which the area has long been renowned. *SP*

Laggan lies roughly 60km north of Goulburn and the Hume Highway via Crookwell on Crookwell then Laggan roads. Taralga is 28km east via mainly gravel road on the Taralga-Laggan Road.

☎ 02 4837 3208   ⊕ www.visitupperlachlan.com.au/lagganvillage

LORD NELSON HOTEL

the rocks, sydney

Another hostelry to boast the moniker of 'Sydney's oldest continually licensed hotel', the Lord Nelson still retains its charm and rustic colonial character.

Originally the home of former convict turned plasterer William Wells, the three storey building was constructed in 1836 of sandstone quarried from nearby Observatory Hill. In 1841 Wells obtained a liquor licence for his then home which was to become the Lord Nelson Hotel.

Through the front doors you are greeted with wide timber floorboards to the bar, the ceilings are held high over-head by huge timber beams. The massive sandstone walls are adorned with memorabilia including a copy of the hotel's first licence. Guestrooms are on the second floor. *SP*

The Lord Nelson is situated in Sydney's Rocks precinct on the corner of Kent Street and Argyle Place. It's within easy walking distance from Wynyard train station and also Circular Quay (bus, train and ferry).

☎ 02 9251 4044 ⊕ www.lordnelsonbrewery.com

ABOVE: Named in honour of Lord Horatio Nelson (1758-1805), a distinguished English naval commander. Nelson was killed during the Battle of Trafalgar off the Spanish coast while leading Britain to a decisive victory over the French Navy during the Napoleonic Wars. The hotel's imposing facade provides an impression of enduring grandeur and is a Sydney landmark.

LEFT: With it's own on-site brewery, many of the pub's beers take their names from the rip-roaring days of Lord Nelson's conquests, boasting titles such as Victory Bitter and Trafalgar Pale Ale, and nautical jargon such as Three Sheets.

THIS PAGE: The pub's bar room still retains it's look and historic feel. From the massive wooden beams, solid sandstone walls and timber floors, it is a welcoming retreat. In winter an open fireplace adds to the bar's ambience. Hanging on the sandstone walls is an original copy of the *Times* newspaper dated 7th November 1805, which details the Battle of Trafalgar and Lord Nelson's death.

MOUNT KEMBLA HOTEL

mount kembla, illawarra

History books show that Mount Kembla Hotel was actually built in 1887 but its licence wasn't confirmed until 1898. It is the oldest remaining weatherboard pub in the Illawarra region and was established in an era dominated by coal mining, presumably to offset the hard working miners from dying of thirst! Mining ceased in 1970 but resumed again in 2003.

Mount Kembla was the site of one of Australia's largest industrial disasters when in July 1902 an explosion, caused by the flame lights used by miners, killed 96 men.

Eerily enough, past publicans believe they have seen or heard the ghost of Michael Brennan in the pub's cellar. Brennan, an underground labourer in the mine at the time of the 1902 disaster, was the only body never found.

The quaint, two storey verandahed building features a long L-shaped main bar, restaurant with both indoor and alfresco dining, lounge/pool room and a large tree shaded beer garden.*SP*

Mount Kembla Village is 8km west of Wollongong on the NSW South Coast and roughly 85km south of Sydney. The hotel is located at 274 Cordeaux Road off the Princes Highway.

☎ **02 4271 1119** ⊕ **www.mkvh.com.au**

PEEL INN

---

nundle, new england

Nestled in the picturesque Peel Valley, the Peel Inn, in the village of Nundle, dates from the 1860s. Constructed during the goldrush days, the inn, which boasts a six meter wide verandah, is the sole survivor of the dozen or so pubs which previously existed in the town. Built by William McIlveen, popular local folklore has it that the hotel was won in a card game from McIlveen by John Schofield, just a few short years after its construction. Schofield's descendants operated the hotel for the next 150 years!

A classic two storey country hotel, it boasts a couple of bars downstairs along with a dining room. Upstairs, and looking out over the wide, timber-floored verandah, are the guestrooms.*CL*

Nundle is 390km north of Sydney via the New England Highway. It is located 60km south-east of Tamworth with access along Nundle Road. The hotel is on Jenkins Street.

☎02 6769 3377 🌐www.peelinn.com.au

ROYAL HOTEL

hill end, central west

Originally one of 28 pubs built in Hill End during the gold rush era, the current Royal Hotel stems from 1872 and is the last remaining of all the hotels in the historic village, which comes under the auspices of the New South Wales National Parks. At its peak, Hill End was home to 10 000 people from all walks of life, many in search of their fortunes. In fact, the largest gold specimen ever discovered was found at Hill End. The Holtermann Nugget was 149cm long, weighed 290kg and contained 93kg of pure gold.

Although the pub has undergone some renovations over the years, the ground floor bar and dining room still retain their colonial-era feel. The front bar room is packed with framed historical photographs and other memorabilia. Upstairs there are 12 guestrooms.

Hill End has been a long-time haunt for some of Australia's best-known artists, with a number living in the village.*CL*

Hill End is 270km north-west of Sydney via the Great Western Highway. It is a little over an hours drive (70km) from Bathurst via Turondale and Hill End roads.

☎ 02 6337 8261 ⊕ www.royalhotelhillend.com

ROYAL HOTEL

---

mount hope, western region

Mount Hope started its days as a mining town after copper ore was discovered there in the 1870s. During the mining boom Mount Hope boasted a population of around 3000. These days a dozen or so people call the town home, with the Royal Hotel or Mount Hope Pub as it's affectionately known, its lifeblood.

The Royal Hotel was first established in 1881 and is believed to have the only concrete bar in NSW. In the 1950s a bushfire roared through the area, destroying most of the town. Ironically, all that remained of the pub was the concrete bar.

The hotel services passing traffic on the Kidman Way between Cobar and Hillston in Central Western NSW. There are both meals and accommodation available. *SP*

Mount Hope is situated in central west NSW roughly 160km south of Cobar and 95km north of Hillston on the Kidman Way.

☎ 02 6897 7988 ⊕ www.facebook.com/Royal-Hotel-Mount-Hope

ROYAL MAIL HOTEL

booroorban, central riverina

Sitting smack, bang in the middle of the vast Old Man Plain, which stretches from Hay south to Wanganella, is the settlement of Booroorban. It now consists of only a pub, the Royal Mail Hotel. Englishman Samuel Porter built the pub in 1868 and it's the last remaining coaching inn on the former Cobb & Co route between Hay and Deniliquin. Booroorban was also on the bullock team route, transporting wool to Echuca and Bendigo. At its peak the busy little town boasted a population of 200.

A local story tells the tale of the Headless Horseman. Drovers who camped just to the south of the pub told of a horseman who appeared at the campsite at Black Swamp, mounted on a trotting cob, a cloak about his shoulders but with no head, spooking the livestock and causing stampedes.

The brick and iron hotel remains much the same today as in its Cobb and Co days. The front bar still retains its unpainted brick walls which add to the rustic feel. The open fire is welcome in winter. Meals are available and camping is possible behind the hotel. *CL*

Booroorban is located 48km south of Hay and 75km north of Deniliquin on the Cobb Highway.

☎ 02 6993 0694 🌐 www.facebook.com/BooroorbanHotel

SETTLERS ARMS INN

st albans, upper hawkesbury

Referred to as the 'forgotten valley', the tiny village of St Albans is home to the historic Settlers Arms Inn and sits on the banks of the Macdonald River.

The two storey convict-built establishment is constructed of sandstone with the first licence being issued in 1836. There is some confusion as to when the building was constructed as land sales in the area didn't start until July 1842 and further documents suggest that the building wasn't completed until a few years after this.

Inside, the hotel offers a glimpse into what life would have been like in the 1800s. In the days of stage coaches, drovers and travellers many stopped by on their way between Sydney and the Hunter Valley.

In the 1930s business slowed and Mrs Jurd, the licencee at the time, called it a day. For the next 30 years it served as the local store, post office and telephone exchange until the 1970s when it was re-licensed, first for takeaway sales then, in 1983, as a hotel. *SP*

St Albans can be accessed from the south via Wisemans Ferry either from Hornsby (70km) through the Galston Gorge or from Windsor (63km). It's approximately a 1½ hour drive north-west of Sydney.

☎ 02 4568 2111 🌐 www.settlersarms.com.au

THIS PAGE: The Settlers Arms Inn's small public bar harks back to its colonial past. Originally known as the Travellers Arms and then Jurd's Hotel, the pub has had a chequered past, but has managed to retain its historical charm of days long gone, including a beer dispensed on a traditional hand pump. The low ceilings and doorways, open fires and massive sandstone walls all add to the hotel's cosy and intimate feel.

ABOVE: Like many historic hotels and inns, objects relating to the local area often adorn the walls, as is the case here at the Settlers Arms. Another feature are the warming open fires.

ABOVE RIGHT: Built in the colonial Georgian style, and although set above the Macdonald River, floodwaters have entered the Settlers Arms on a couple of occasions. The flood of 1889, the worst in the valley's history, rose almost to the hotel's eaves!

RIGHT: The hotel serves meals and offers accommodation, making it a popular day and weekend destination from both Sydney, the Central Coast and Hunter Valley.

SURVEYOR GENERAL INN

berrima, southern highlands

The Surveyor General Inn, in the historic southern highlands village of Berrima, was built of convict-hewn sandstone in 1834 by William Harper and first licensed by his son James. The Harper family owned the inn for close to a century. The cellar was once used to lock-up convicts until a gaol was built nearby a few years later.

The pub's fortunes have waxed and waned over its 170 plus year history. In the 1960s the Surveyor General's condition had declined so badly that it was to be knocked down. Fortunately through dedicated fund raising efforts, the village of Berrima including the Surveyor General Inn, was restored to its former glory. The Surveyor General Inn lays claim to being 'Australia's oldest continuously licensed inn'.

The Inn's original taproom still functions as the main bar, with stone walls, timber and pressed metal ceilings, open fireplaces and an 80 year old carved cedar bar. There are four guestrooms.*SP*

The Suryeyor General Inn is in the historic village of Berrima in the southern highlands. Berrima is 120km south-west of Sydney and 72km north-east of Goulburn via the Hume Highway.

☎ 02 4877 1226 🌐 www.surveyorgeneralinn.com.au

THE LOADED DOG HOTEL

tarago, southern tablelands

The two storey brick and granite hotel was established in 1848 and known as the Lake Bathurst Hotel. It was later rebadged sometime in the early twentieth century after the hilarious Henry Lawson short story, *The Loaded Dog,* which portrays the exploits of three goldminers, their dog and a misguided idea of catching fish with explosives.

Legend has it that infamous bushranger Frank Gardiner called a meeting in the early 1860s, inviting fellow bushrangers Ben Hall and the Clarke Brothers to plan a major gold heist. During discussions an argument errupted between Hall's men, a pistol was drawn and fired - with fatal consequences. It is said that the body of hotel patron Johnny Keith, an innocent bystander, was buried under the floorboards near the fireplace.

The corrugated iron roofed building features open fireplaces, dining room, accommodation, beer garden, main bar and decorative pressed metal ceilings. It is a popular weekend day trip destination from Canberra. *SP*

Tarago is located 42km south of Goulburn via the Braidwood Road and from Braidwood its roughly 50km north via the Kings Highway then Braidwood Road. Canberra is about 65km west of Tarago via Bungendore.

☏ **02 4849 4499** ⊕ **www.loadeddoghotel.com**

THE LORD DUDLEY HOTEL

woollahra, sydney

The Lord Dudley Hotel began its days as the Underwood Estate Hotel circa 1890. It was named after emancipated convict James Underwood who owned much of the land which was later to became the suburb of Paddington. The current hotel dates from 1908.

The pub was popular with local quarrymen who lived in the surrounding terrace houses and worked the nearby sandstone quarry while Les Darcy, the famous Australian boxer, had a part-time job at the Lord Dudley after he moved to Sydney.

An English-style pub comprising of three levels, it is built of brick and features an Edwardian timber bar on entering off the street. Pressed metal ceilings, dartboard, open fireplace and timber furniture fill the rest of the ground floor and lounge area. The restaurant/dining makes up the basement. The hotel boasts a mixed bag of clientele from local high flyers to back-packing Poms seeking a taste of home.*SP*

The Lord Dudley is situated in the affluent Paddington/Woollahra area in Sydney's eastern suburbs. It sits on the corner of Quarry Street and Jersey Road about 3km from the city centre.

☏ 02 9327 5399 ⊕ www.lorddudley.com.au

THE NEATH HOTEL

neath, lower hunter valley

Spanning three storeys, The Neath Hotel was established in 1914 in the former coal mining village of Neath. Situated next to the railway line, the pub soon became a popular stop-off for miners on their way home from the pits.

A story now enshrined in local folklore is that of Harry Littlefair and his miner's lamp. Harry was a local coal miner and hotel patron who, before departing for overseas with the Australian Imperial Force in World War I, left his brass miner's lamp and oil tin in the care of the hotel's landlady, to be collected on his return. Sadly, Harry was killed in action in France and his lamp has remained behind the bar of The Neath Hotel ever since. Every ANZAC day Harry's lamp is lit to commemorate Harry and all the others who never returned.

The largest building of its kind in the area, the hotel features a grand foyer, public bar and dining rooms on the ground floor. The first and second floors consist of guestrooms. *SP*

Neath is located between Cessnock and Kurri Kurri in the Lower Hunter Valley, roughly 6km east of Cessnock and 9km west of Kurri Kurri.

☎ **02 4930 8739** ⊕ **www.theneathhotel.com.au**

THE SIR GEORGE

jugiong, hilltops

A substantial two storey building boasting locally quarried granite walls up to half a meter thick, The Sir George was built in 1845, but closer to the river then where she now lies. The original hotel, along with the rest of the town, was washed away in 1852 when the nearby Murrumbidgee River flooded. John Sheahan, an Irish-settler and owner of the hotel, brought stonemasons over from Ireland to carry out the work of rebuilding the hotel, this time a little further back from the river! The hotel remained in the Sheahan family until 2014.

The hotel was once a popular coach stop on the Hume Highway in the early horse and cart days. During the goldrush era, the area was an easy target for holdups. In 1864 bushrangers Ben Hall, Johnny Gilbert and John Dunn held up a mail coach between Gundagai and Jugiong, and after a gunfight, escaped with a substantial booty of gold.

The hotel underwent extensive period sympathetic renovations in 2016. *SP*

The Sir George lies off the Hume Highway on the banks of the Murrumbidgee River in Jugiong, 65km west of Yass and 42km north-east of Gundagai. The pub is on the Old Hume Highway (Riverside Drive).

☎ **0419 098 828** 🌐 **www.sirgeorge.com.au**

TOOMA INN

---

tooma, snowy mountains

Built by Charles Woodhouse circa 1884, the single storey building was constructed from handmade bricks baked on site. Designed in the Georgian colonial style, it contained seven rooms with a detached kitchen and laundry at the rear – which were later connected in 1912 – and large cellar beneath the hotel. Woodhouse also had interests in hotels in Tumbarumba and Jingellic.

There was a time during the mid 1900s when the hotel operated illegally. Seems that the publican at the time got waylaid during his trip to Tumbarumba to renew the hotel's licence, but seen as a 'good bloke' the lapsed licence was overlooked until it was renewed the following year!

Today, the pub has a public bar, dining room as well as three guestrooms. There is a beer garden out the back.

At one time Tooma was in the race to be the nation's capital, but in the 1908 ballot it drew a short straw and was eliminated from the contest, which was eventually awarded to Canberra. *CL*

Tooma is located 34km south of Tumbarumba on the Tooma Road and 40km north-east of Corryong via Welaregang.

☎ 02 6948 4012 🌐 www.facebook.com/The-Tooma-Inn

TRUNDLE HOTEL

---

trundle, central west

The first Trundle Hotel was established in 1888. In 1911 Evan Jones purchased the hotel and set about rebuilding it to offer accommodation to travellers. The two storey hotel is constructed of a mixture of rendered brick and rammed earth with corrugated iron roofing, featuring a bullnose iron covered timber verandah which spans over 80m in length.

Inside, the pub features a main bar downstairs, large dining room and accommodation upstairs. Pressed metal walls and ceilings feature throughout. The hotel is listed on the Register of the National Estate.

Trundle's claim to fame is its main street, which at over 60m wide, is the widest in New South Wales. Once a busy stock route, it was constructed to accommodate three (3) chains of bullock teams passing through. The wide main street would also allow the teamsters to turn around and park their teams outside the hotel.*SP*

Trundle is on the Bogan Way, roughly 60km north-west of Parkes and 75km north-east of Condobolin via Bogan Gate. It is 140km south-west of Dubbo off the Newell Highway.

☎ 02 6892 1009 🌐 **www.trundlehotel.com.au**

THIS PAGE: Located on the pub's ground floor is the main public bar. It was here in 1900 that Trundle's resident physician, Dr Dagmar Berne, died on the spot where the bar now stands. Having risen from her sick bed - she had suffered from tuberculosis for many years - to tend to a hotel patron who had injured himself, the good doctor, shortly after attending to the patron, died from a pulmonary haemorrhage. She was 34 years old. Dr Berne, who was the first female to study medicine and the fourth woman to become a registered doctor in Australia, is now the 'patron' saint of the Trundle Hotel.

ABOVE: Boasting the second longest pub verandah in New South Wales at a shade over 87 metres long, it offers a great vantage point to take in the views out and over the widest main street in the state, at 60 metres in width!

RIGHT: The street-level entry is well protected by the hotel's massive verandah. The outside walls, as well as some of the pub's interior, features numerous original brewery and beer advertising signs. Many of these proudly show their age, which adds to the character of the place.

VICTORIA HOTEL

moonan flat, upper hunter

Erected on the banks of the Upper Hunter River in the late 1860s, the historic Victoria Hotel is a quaint reminder of the area's rip-roaring gold-rush days. Originally a stopover on a stage coaching route, it was first licensed as a hotel by Margaret Mitchell in 1898. Over the years it has been frequented by miners, bushrangers, farmers and now, increasingly, by travellers exploring the delightful Upper Hunter region.

The infamous bushranger Fredrick Ward, alias Captain Thunderbolt, is said to have robbed two miners at Denison Diggings, as Moonan Flat was then known, in February 1867 and it is often quoted that he fired a pistol shot into the ceiling of the pub's bar, which it is said remained visible for many years until it was painted over.

Outside is a shaded beer garden beneath an ancient pine tree while inside contains the bar area, complete with a warming open fire. The dining room is in the adjacent building. The pub also has accommodation. *CL*

Moonan Flat is 50km north-east of Scone with access via Gundy Road. Access is also possible from the east via Barrington Tops Road from Gloucester, but check road conditions first.

☎ 02 6546 3165 ⊕ www.victoriahotelmoonanflat.webs.com

BOILING BILLY

A licensed imprint to Woodslane Press, 10 Apollo Street, Warriewood NSW 2102 Australia
Email: info@woodslane.com.au | Tel: 02 8445 2300 | www.woodslane.com.au

This 1st edition 2018
Copyright © text Craig Lewis and Simon Punch 2018, Copyright © Photographs Craig Lewis | Boiling Billy Images 2018
Copyright © Photographs Simon Punch 2018

ISBN: 9781925403909

Book design and layout: Craig Lewis | Boiling Billy Publications
Editing and proofreading: Cathy Savage | Boiling Billy Publications
Printed in China by Asia Pacific Offset

A catalogue record for this
book is available from the
National Library of Australia

Boiling Billy Publications welcomes feedback from readers. If you would like to get in touch then please write or e-mail us at: Boiling Billy Publications, Nimmitabel NSW 2631 | E-mail: info@boilingbilly.com.au
Web: www.boilingbilly.com.au | www.facebook.com/boilingbilly | Tel: 02 6454 6162

Craig Lewis: is the author of numerous Australiana books, including the perennial favourite *Australian Bush Pubs*. He has been travelling, camping out, photographing and writing about his adventures for the past 20 or so years. He lives in the New South Wales High Country.

Simon Punch: is a keen surfer and photographer who lives on the New South Wales South Coast with his wife and growing family. He is also the author of *Surfing New South Wales – the essential guide for the travelling surfer*.